This journal belongs to

....

Contact info

....

....

....

Date

....

This is a new day.

I'm going to receive God's mercy.

Introduction

You were created to be filled with joy, peace, confidence, and creativity. But it's easy to go through life holding on to things that weigh you down—guilt, resentment, doubt, worry. When you allow these negative emotions in, they take up space that you need for the good things that move you toward your destiny.

Along with the book *Empty Out the Negative*, this journal is meant to help you train yourself to release any negative thoughts and feelings from the day and to put on a fresh new attitude every morning. Discover encouraging, inspirational thoughts from the book that serve as daily reminders of how you can power up and get your mind going in the right direction. All are provided to engage you in a process of reflection that will enhance your faith and help you to rise to new levels of being your best.

Let this be an open door to self-discovery and a record of your daily progress as you begin the journey toward living the life you were born to live. God promises that if you will make room for the good things, you'll step into all the new things He has in store for you!

Don't look at how big the problem is; look at how big your God is.

If you don't set the tone for the day, negative thoughts will set it for you.

Your attitude can make up for a lack of experience, a lack of training, and a lack of talent.

If you're going to be an eagle, if you're going to soar, you can't go back to the dead things in your life that will poison you.

....
....
....
....
....
....
....
....
....
....
....
....
....
....
....
....
....
....
....
....
....
....
....
....
....
....

You may be a product of your past, but you don't have to be
a prisoner of your past.

The reason the Scripture says to "leave it" is because
you're going to be tempted to pick it back up.

The more you dwell on the right thoughts, the less room there is for the wrong thoughts.

The way you see yourself is the way other people are going to see you.

You don't have to spend another minute being infected by wrong thinking.

No matter how good a seed is, its growth is dependent on having good soil.

Find people who will fan your flame, not people
who will throw water on your flame.

Life is too short for you to live with negative things holding you down.

You were created to be filled with joy, peace, confidence, and creativity.

You need people who will help pull you into your destiny.

If you let go of the questions of life, you will have a peace
that goes beyond what you can understand.

Tune out your defeated thoughts and think power thoughts. "Something good is going to happen to me. Favor is surrounding me like a shield. Goodness and mercy are following me."

When God created you, He put in you everything you need to fulfill your destiny.

Your thoughts set the limits for your life.

Let go of the disappointments of yesterday, let go of what didn't work out,
and get your mind going in the right direction.

God will fight your battles.

....

....

....

....

....

....

....

....

....

....

....

....

....

....

....

....

....

....

....

....

....

....

....

This is a new day. There are new victories, new relationships,
and new opportunities.

God doesn't waste the struggles you've survived,
but you're not supposed to feed off them.

There's a new beginning in front of you.

If you get rid of that negative baggage, you'll not only feel a weight lift off you, but you'll step into the new things God has in store.

Receive this into your spirit: Better is coming. Healing is coming, breakthroughs are coming, and new opportunities are coming.

God has given you a gift. He could have created someone else to be alive on this day and at this time, but He chose you.

God will heal your hurts. He'll restore your broken pieces.

Joy is coming, healing is coming, favor is coming,
the fullness of your destiny is coming.

....

....

....

....

....

....

....

....

....

....

....

....

....

....

....

....

....

....

....

....

....

....

....

....

It's going to take boldness to believe that you're amazing, you're marvelous, and you're wonderfully made.

When the negative comes up, do yourself a favor and delete it.
Switch over to the right recording.

The enemy wouldn't be trying to stop you if he didn't know
there was something amazing in your future.

Just as the wrong people will pull you down, the right people will pull you up.

God is ready to fill your life with good things.

....
....
....
....
....
....
....
....
....
....
....
....
....
....
....
....
....
....
....
....
....
....
....
....
....
....

You may not understand why it happened, but the Scripture says,
"God will give us a peace that passes understanding."

Get out of the *was* and come over into the *is*.

Don't let a sour attitude keep you grounded.
It's time to rise to new levels, to soar to new heights.

....

....

....

....

....

....

....

....

....

....

....

....

....

....

....

....

....

....

....

....

....

....

....

....

....

Nothing that has happened to you was a surprise to God.

You may have had a rough start, but you don't have to have a rough finish.
Better is the end.